Adrian Bradbury

Illustrated by Steven Wood

Would You Rather?

Lou Kuenzler

Illustrated by Alan Brown

OXFORD
UNIVERSITY PRESS

Great Clarendon Street, Oxford, OX2 6DP, United Kingdom

Oxford University Press is a department of the University of Oxford. It furthers the University's objective of excellence in research, scholarship, and education by publishing worldwide. Oxford is a registered trade mark of Oxford University Press in the UK and in certain other countries.

Text © Oxford University Press 2025

Illustrations © Steven Wood and Alan Brown 2025

The moral rights of the author have been asserted

First published in 2025

All rights reserved. No part of this publication may be reproduced, stored in a retrieval system, transmitted, used for text and data mining, or used for training artificial intelligence, in any form·or by any means, without the prior permission in writing of Oxford University Press, or as expressly permitted by law, by licence or under terms agreed with the appropriate reprographics rights organization. Enquiries concerning reproduction outside the scope of the above should be sent to the Rights Department, Oxford University Press, at the address above.

You must not circulate this work in any other form and you must impose this same condition on any acquirer

British Library Cataloguing in Publication Data
Data available

ISBN: 978-1-382-05303-7

10 9 8 7 6 5 4 3 2 1

The manufacturing process conforms to the environmental regulations of the country of origin.

Printed in China by Golden Cup

Acknowledgements

Robot School written by Adrian Bradbury; *Would You Rather?* written by Lou Kuenzler

The publisher would like to thank Activity Alliance for their valuable contribution to the development of this book.

The publisher and authors would like to thank the following for permissions to use copyright material:
Front cover: Steven Wood
Back cover: Alan Brown, Steven Wood

Every effort has been made to contact copyright holders of material reproduced in this book. Any omissions will be rectified in subsequent printings if notice is given to the publisher.

Contents

Robot School   5

Would You Rather?   19

Green words

Single-syllable words

pr**ou**d   m**ou**th   **air**   z**oo**m   fl**oor**   sc**ore**   f**ir**st

Multi-syllabic words

add|ress   **ou**t|d**oor**s   less|on   pres|ent
San|j**ay**   th**ir**|ty

Root words and suffixes

del**ay** → del**ay**ed   fast → fastest
travel → travel**ling**

....

Red words

y(our)   d(ow)n   s(ch)ool   n(ow)   s(o)me

....

Challenge words

tea**ch**ers   **eye**s   open   try   robot   data

ROBOT SCHOOL

Mount Street School is now open.

The teachers are all robots!

"Good morning," bleeps the teacher. "I am teacher B9364B. That's a mouthful, so you may address me as Miss B9. Let us begin our first lesson."

"Are you going to check we are all present, Miss?" Sanjay asks.

Miss B9 whirls around. "Thank you Sanjay Kapoor but I do not need to. I have scanned your eyes and logged them into this morning's data bank."

Maths is next. Olly puts his hand up. He wants to get out of Maths.

Olly Pound ... Born: 10th May.

Siblings: three. Keen on tennis and Scouts.

Last maths test score: 22 out of 30.

Your right hand is in the air.

The class go outdoors for PE.

Miss B9 dips into her skills data bank and picks which sports they will do. Sanjay is given tag rugby, which he loves.

The class plays three sports. Miss B9 refs all three. Thirty kids whizz around her as she shouts commands without missing a thing.

Sanjay spins the ball. He astounds himself by scoring the winning try!

"That was an **outstanding** try, Sanjay," says Miss B9. "You will be a rugby star one day, with some adjustments to your play."

Sanjay feels so proud.

Maybe having a robot teacher isn't so bad.

Green words

Single-syllable words

point   spoil   score   fair

Multi-syllabic words

ann|oy   dis|a|ppoint   a|ssem|bly   mass|ive
el|e|phant   con|test

Root words and suffixes

destroy → destroyed   hard → hardest
avoid → avoiding   end → endless

....

Red words

love   her   would   school   watch   everyone

....

Challenge words

rather   again   like   dance   jokes
never   always   whisper

Would You Rather?

Toya loves to annoy her twin, Zak. Zak enjoys annoying her, too!

They play an endless contest of **'Would you rather?'**.

So Zak, **would you rather** be extra fast or extra strong?

Extra fast! Then I can outrun you on the football pitch!

No way!

I have a good one, Sis! **Would you rather** never play football again? Or you have to *pay* a thousand pounds to score in your next match?

£1000

Do you have to ask? I'd pay the cash. I am too good at football to disappoint all my fans. Did I tell you I scored a hat-trick last night?

Hmm, let me think. Yes, you did. You have not shut up about it! But how will you get a thousand pounds? You just have three coins in your coin box.

Fair point!

What about you, Zak? **Would you rather** sound like a sheep when you chat in school? Or sound like a noisy frog when you sing with your band?

I'd pick the sheep. Frog-singing would spoil our best hits.

Would you rather be an extra-small elephant or a massive rat?

A little elephant would be so sweet! No, hang on! I would be a massive rat. I'd enjoy squirming out of your school bag to give you a fright.

Would you rather always shout or always whisper?

Always shout! I love being noisy.

Right, kids. I'm off to join that ballroom dance club in Royal Hill.

Gulp!

Would you rather have fish and chips or curry tonight?

Glossary

Robot School

astounds: shocks

data bank: where lots of information is stored

logged: saved

refs (referees): makes sure everyone follows the rules

Scouts: a club where children can do lots of different activities

siblings: children with the same parent

try: getting the ball over the line in rugby

Would You Rather?

hat-trick: score three goals